WHAT YOUR LAB IS THINKING

WHAT YOUR LAB IS THINKING

WILLOW CREEK PRESS®

Published by Willow Creek Press, Inc.
P.O. Box 147, Minocqua, Wisconsin 54548

Printed in China

Now remember, smile like you didn' just tear up the couch.

Wait a second? You tricked me! You told me we were going for a car ride. You didn't say anything about the vet.

So what's the worst they could do to me?

In my defense, you didn't tell me to NOT go into the mud.

Your bed?
You mean my bed.
Get your own.

I'll just wait here and guard the door.

Hello, pleasure to meet you shorty.
Now don't mess with me.

I always get shotgun.

Oh, you're going on vacation? I could use a vacation. Take me!

For my next trick, I need your favorite slippers.

I haven't eaten in an hour, that's 7 in dog hours.

Code Red: Neighborhood cat entering yard... Battle stations!

Fur missile incoming!!!

I'm lucky
I'm so cute.

Oooh yeah, bring it on!

Right, I'm "not allowed" on the furniture. Got it.

No, I haven't seen the donuts. Why do you ask?

I'm not saying I'm the most beautiful Lab in the world, but you certainly can.

Look Ma, no hands.

That's it, come just two steps closer. Now... watch this!

The force is strong with this one.

I got a good one to throw at the cat!

Hey, could someone give me a little help here?

I hate you and this cone.

How about I take you for a walk? Looks like you put on a few pounds.

I got this!

Yes, I drank out of the toilet.
You do what in there?!

Okay, this is nice and peaceful and all, but if that duck swims five feet closer things are going to get crazy.

Maybe if I drool on your lap you will give me food.

Don't you dare Snapchat me...
That's an invasion of privacy.

No, I'm gonna beat you.
No, I'm gonna beat you.
No, I'm gonna beat you.

He had it coming.

Why must you talk to me like I'm an infant? I'm 91 years old in dog years.

Oh, We're sorry.
Did you like this ball?

Throwing the ball isn't that difficult when I'm the one chasing it.

Why is there a tree in the house if I can't pee on it?

Neuter? What the heck does that mean?

Alexa, order more dog food.

How about you go outside in the rain and see if you like it?

Ewe, did you just fart?
Oh wait, that was me.

Please throw this ball 100 more times.

I got a novel idea. How about next time you just throw the ball on land?

I'm teething and it hurts. Please don't yell at me for chewing everything.

Oh hey, you're home early. I was just straightening up.

Make way, I heard the fridge open!

Cute is just my cover!

When Labs take over this planet you'll be punished for what you're doing to me.

This is quite pedestrian. I was hoping for a bone-in ribeye with an au poivre sauce.

Snowball, huh? Not funny.
Not funny at all.

Can you turn on Animal Planet? The Puppy Bowl is this Sunday!

I love it when the mailman plays fetch with me.

Here, let me help you with the groceries.

Stop staring at us. We are trying to remember Plan B.

Why am I out here and the cat's in there?

I found a little stick for you to throw.

Sup sista...
You new to the hood?

Was that thunder? I heard thunder. Did you hear thunder? That was definitely thunder.

Down the chimney? Really?

Can we go for a walk again, please? I got the hots for the Chihuahua down the street.

Wanna play with me?

I smell bacon!
I want bacon!

If you Instagram this, so help me, I will pee in your shoes!

It was me, I let the dogs out.

I got it. No, I got it. No really, I got it.
I got it. No, I got it. No really, I got it.

Does this angle make me look fat?

I'm just gonna help with the gardening.

There's alway one in the family that ruins every picture.

auto Winter
75 Jahre Autohaus Winter
Auto Winter
zum 75-jährigen Jubiläum
LUDWIGSBURGER KREISZEITUNG

Have I got news for you!

I detect a hint of chicken flavor with subtle overtones of beef. Smooth finish. A good bone, but not a great bone.

No, I don't feel like going for a run. My legs are half the size of yours.

What? If you would have paid attention to me instead of your cell phone this wouldn't have happened.

I think we need to send this food to the LAB for testing.

Yes I'm large, but I want to be a lap dog. Don't you have dreams?

Zip-a-dee-friggin-
doo-da!!!

Why don't you make the cat do this? I look like an idiot.

I hate this white stuff. It sticks to my fur and my butt is cold.

...can't...keep...
eyes...open...
ZZZZZZZZZZZZZ

This is for letting the cat pee in the house.

Cannonball!!!!

Slow down, it's not a race.
Wait a second, it IS a race!

I need to find my inner Zen.

You're my best friend.
You're my best friend too.